Flying at Lanark

Ed Archer

This photograph is not only important for showing Armstrong Drexel in flight in his Bleriot but it also shows the stands and one of the marquees which were erected for the Lanark International Aviation Meeting. The stands alone cost about £5,000 to erect and in themselves they cost more than was raised by local subscription. The preparations for the great event including laying more than nine miles of telegraph cabling to enable essential communications to the outside world. This was vital for the Press Corps attending the meeting, also in case of any emergencies.

First published in the United Kingdom, 2010,
by Stenlake Publishing Ltd
01290 551122
www.stenlake.co.uk
ISBN 9781840335019

Printed by Walker and Connell Ltd
01560 320237
www.WalkerandConnell.co.uk

Above and below left: Percy Pilcher had a great interest in aviation which he developed whilst an assistant lecturer at Glasgow University . He first of all experimented with a variety of gliders which had a limited capacity for lift; his best glider could only lift up 0.7 lbs. per square foot. Realising the limitations of his gliders, he got to work on the development of an aero engine. Once built he took it down to Stanford Hall, near Market Harborough in Leicestershire, but the engine did not perform so he decided to give the crowd of onlookers a demonstration of the capabilities of his glider. It broke up and Percy Pilcher died as a result of his injuries on 2nd October 1899. Percy Pilcher is the forgotten hero of Scottish aviation.

Right: The crash landing of Louis Bleriot after crossing the Channel on 28th July 1909 was to stimulate an interest in aviation amongst the British public. The original post card of this event was produced within 24 hours of the Channel crossing. Not everybody was impressed by this achievement; Louis' wife made him promise not to fly again. However, he did fly again, at Reims, in late August in what was to be the world's first International air show. After the show Bleriot decided it was a better idea to concentrate on aircraft design.

Introduction

My interest in aviation stretches back to my childhood. At the age of eleven I was an avid reader both of *Flight* magazine and the *Meccano* Magazine, but it was not until I was in my forties that I became interested in air shows and aircraft museums. Then ten years ago I thought that the Lanark International Aviation Meeting of 1910 should be celebrated. At that time there was little interest in doing anything to mark the events of 1910. However, in the past two years I have been actively involved as a member of the Lanark Air Show Centenary Committee in trying to organise events and interest people in the contribution Lanark made to aviation history.

The research that I did to find out the story behind the postcards issued for the 1910 meeting forms the basis for this book. Early on I found out that over 200,000 people visited the Lanark meeting and that figure grabbed my imagination. Why? Many people had never seen an aeroplane and the meeting was an opportunity to see something as exciting as the Moon Landing was to my generation in 1969.

The beginnings of military interest in planes was stirring and their potential was explored at Lanark. In 1909 Winston Churchill had declared that future military campaigns would be decided by who had mastery of the skies. Two British companies responded to this challenge and they both had planes at Lanark. The British and Colonial Aviation Company (later Bristol Aviation) had their Bristol Boxkite adopted by the military. The other company present was Shorts, who ended up supplying their seaplane to the Royal Navy.

The Lanark International Aviation Meeting was regarded as having been the most successful air show of 1910 and one of the best in the world. This reputation kept Lanark on the map in aviation circles until 1935 when the last aviation event, which was organised by Sir Alan Cobham, took place at Lanark Race Course. This inspired many young people to take up flying, either with civil aviation companies or with the RAF.

Ed Archer - March 2010

Acknowledgements

First and foremost my wife Sandra, who has had to put up with my hermit-like lifestyle. The following people have been kind enough to lend me material – Dugald Cameron, Ken Norris, Ken Liddell. Lanark Library has helped by providing pictures of the posters of the flying circuses. Lanark Museum Trust has been of considerable assistance in providing photographs. Andy Robertson and Donald Malcolm provided the initial inspiration. Richard Stenlake and Paul Archibald helped with material, advice and support to get this book printed. Lewis Hutton for his work designing the book and working on the photographs. Finally I wish to thank the members of the Lanark centenary Aviation Committee and Gill Howie and Berry Vissers of Squadron Prints.

A picture from the *Aero* shows a theodolite in action. The Scottish Aeronautical Society decided to use these as well as barographs to measure the altitude reached by planes at Lanark. Professor Barr, President of the Royal Aeronautical Society was of the opinion that the barograph in the plane gave a more accurate reading.

Left: Charles Rolls (27th August 1877 – 12th July 1910) was one of the first aviation pioneers and he was a prime mover in organising air shows in Britain. Indeed he was a founding member of the Royal Aero Club and the second person in the UK to have a flying certificate. In 1907 he tried to get Frederick Royce to design an aero engine. Royce was not interested and so Rolls spent his time modifying Wright fliers. He was the first Briton to make the double non-stop crossing of the English Channel which took him just 95 minutes, achieved on 2nd June 1910. Just a month later Charles Rolls became the first British aviator to die when his plane broke up at Bournemouth Air Show. But his legacy lived on and the air show that he had helped to plan for Lanark took place in August 1910.

Right: A photo of the dignitaries during preparations for the 1910 Lanark air show taken on 6th August 1910. The prime movers were the Lord Provost of Glasgow, McInnes Shaw; Professor Archibald Barr of the Department of Engineering at Glasgow University; J.H Biles, Professor of Naval Architecture also at Glasgow; R.Maclean, Provost of Glasgow; and Mr R.J. Smith, Secretary of the Scottish Automobile Club. These men along with others got together the funding to take forward the project. Some was raised from guarantors to take care of any loses and others contributed through a subscribers' list

Right: The picture is taken from a programme for the Lanark International Aviation meeting and shows a selection of the competitors who were amongst the 22 aviators who had put their name down for the meeting. Since a programme had to be produced some time before the event, the aviators shown in the programme might not necessarily take part. This is indeed the case as although shown on this photograph Barnes did not appear. Another air show, at Blackpool, commenced before and finished after Lanark. Barnes decided to stay at Blackpool, a poor decision as very little flying was done and no records were broken there.

Below: This Daily News magnum post card was made before the show took place and shows thirteen aviators who had put their name down for Lanark. It contains several errors and some of the aviators' names are incorrectly spelled. It also shows Tetard who, like Barnes, chose to remain at the air show at Blackpool. Neither man enjoyed the success they might have had at Lanark.

Both pictures courtesy Lanark Museum Collection.

The hangars were built prior to the arrival of the aviators and were quite spacious compared with hangars elsewhere. The word 'hangars', however, would have meant little to the general public as hangars were originally described as 'garages'. The hangars were just part of the infrastructure put in place for the air show. Pylons had to be erected for the aviators to go around and a special hut for the timekeeper was made. *Lower left*: The course was marked out and lines were placed on the ground for the aviators to line up prior to taking off. *Lower right*: An information board was also erected.

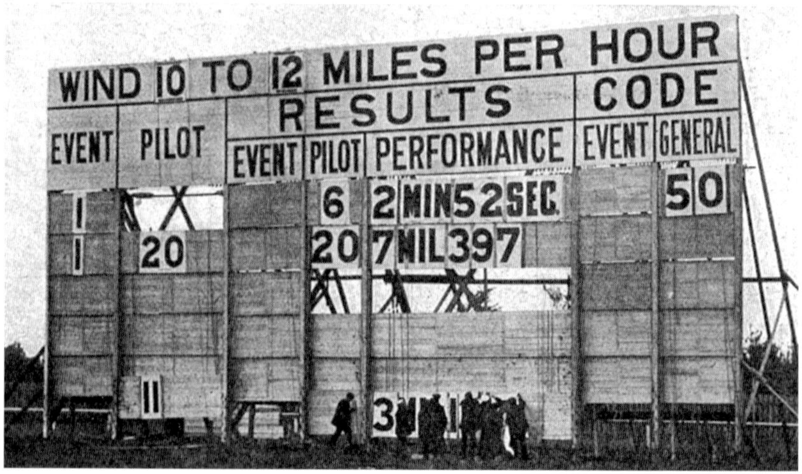

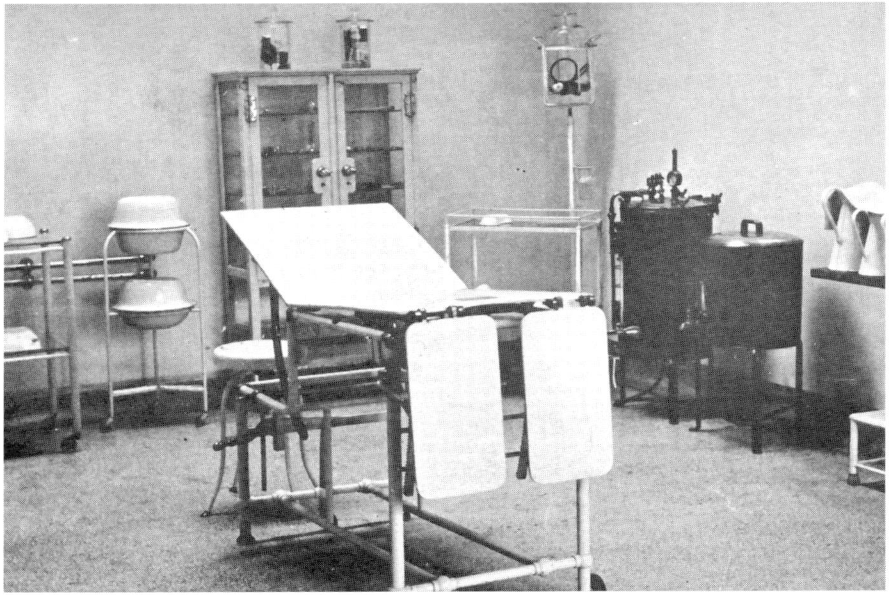

Above: Lanark Race Course had no station until it was seen as necessary for transporting people to the air show. Lanark Race Course Station cost £5,000 and was built in less than six months. This included the installation of a new telegraph office and the creation of a new signalling system. The cost of the station was reimbursed due to the number of visitors coming to Lanark for the International Aviation Week. Literally thousands of people came; their travel plans had to be carefully managed and new timetables created especially for passengers travelling first class. Fourteen special trains were assigned to Lanark alone.The picture of the station shows that it was gradually falling apart by the late 1950s. By the early 1960s the race course station was living on borrowed time and the Beeching cuts were responsible for its eventual destruction.

Left: The operating table in St. Mary's Hospital, Lanark. This hospital was operated by the Roman Catholic church in Lanark and was in 1910 the most up-to-date hospital in Lanark. The Church of St. Mary's Lanark had just been totally rebuilt as a result of a disastrous fire and alongside the church a new hospital had been built. Six beds were reserved in the hospital for the aviators in case of accidents but they were not used. The Lanark aviation meeting was one of the safest that took place in 1910 as there were no deaths!

A variety of enclosures were constructed for paying visitors to the air show . The tickets shown here are the ten shilling, four shilling and two shilling ones. The dearer tickets gave access to the stands which afforded a better view of the proceedings. A number of turnstiles were erected to assist with admission to the show. The best attendance figure was for Wednesday 10th August with a crowd of over 50,000. Not all the entrance money ended up in the right hands, as £68 in half sovereigns disappeared, with apparently both the thief and the collector of the gate money over-refreshed. This crime was never solved.

Tickets courtesy Lanark Museum Collection.

Left: The souvenir industry in Lanark went into full swing prior to the aviation meeting. Lanark did not want to be forgotten so a special shell shaped postcard was designed with a Bleriot monoplane on the front. Inside the shell was held a concertina like pullout of pictures. More than one version was sold, some had pictures of Lanark, others had pictures of planes.

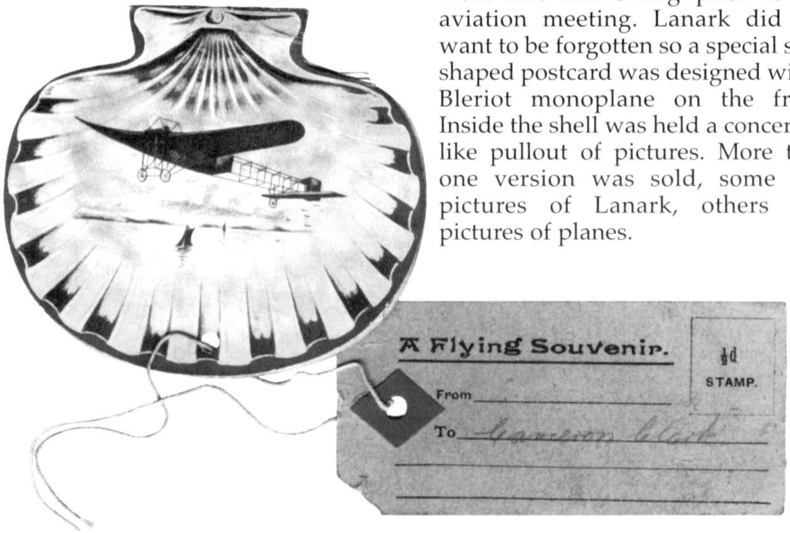

Above: Before the air show took place a post office, postcards' shop and booth for people wishing to have their photograph taken in a mock-up plane were installed. Official photographers were appointed such as the company of Brown and Sons of Lanark and press accreditation was dealt with. This postcard was produced prior to the show but not too much in advance as the main stands had been erected but not the enclosures for the cheap ticket holders. It was appropriate that Radley is shown as he was the first aviator to fly a considerable distance over the Scottish mainland on 4th June 1910. However, he was not the first Scottish aviator; that honour went to Baird.

This postcard purports to show the Frenchman, Gustav Blondeau in flight but in fact it was faked up. Many of the postcards sold at Lanark and indeed at other early aviation shows were scissors and paste jobs. In this case an aircraft claiming association with Blondeau was added. Blondeau's Farman biplane was not particularly successful in helping him to gain prizes though he did get a £10 prize for coming third on the first day of the competition. He covered just over 26 miles. He also took several passengers up on the first day and according to *Flight* he was the first person to do this in Scotland, the *Aero,* on the other hand, claimed that Captain Dickson had that honour.

Right top and centre: Captain Cody was one of the more colourful characters at Lanark. He was involved in the earliest experiments to develop a military aircraft and worked on Military Aircraft No. 1 at Farnborough although this proved to be a disaster. The rather ungainly aircraft Cody brought to Lanark was known as 'the cathedral' due to its size. Due to the fact that it only took off once, it was nicknamed the 'daisy cutter'. Cody realised it was seriously underpowered and fitted two engines to it, but that did not resolve the problem.

Left: This picture from the *Aero* shows Cody tuning up. He was very proud of his own design of aircraft and even inspired others to emulate him. His mechanic, Erik Addyman from Harrogate, decided in 1910 to build a plane for himself but his mother was horrified. She had the servants burn Erik's plane in the garden.

George Chavez was Peruvian though born in France. Both his parents were Peruvian and so he was the only South American to take part in the air show. He had made quite a name for himself at Blackpool where he smashed the world altitude record, climbing to 2,500 feet. Chavez's trip to Lanark was marred by the news that his plane had been burnt in a fire whilst being transported to Lanark. The accident was caused by sparks from the engine pulling the London and North Western Railway Company's train.This portrait of Chavez shows a determined man who was anxious to succeed. He borrowed several planes whilst at Lanark . Gibbs lent him a Farman initially, but really Chavez felt more at home with Gibb's Bleriot which he used to make an attempt on the altitude record on Monday 8th August. His position was sighted by theodolite but the barographs gave a better reading. He got up to over 6,000 feet but the wet and cold weather defeated him.

This picture from the *Aero* of 17th August 1910 shows Blondeau's Farman being tested prior to take-off. This particular flight on Monday 8th August ended fairly abruptly as Blondeau lost control of his Farman and he let it drop thirty feet. Surprisingly enough he emerged unscathed, although after this he did not fly for the rest of the week.

Blondeau is shown in this picture flying around the route laid out on the race course, passing what were referred to at the time as 'pylons'. These pylons were laid out to guide the aviators around the one and a half mile course. Competitions took place as to who could fly around the course slowest and actually stay in the air!

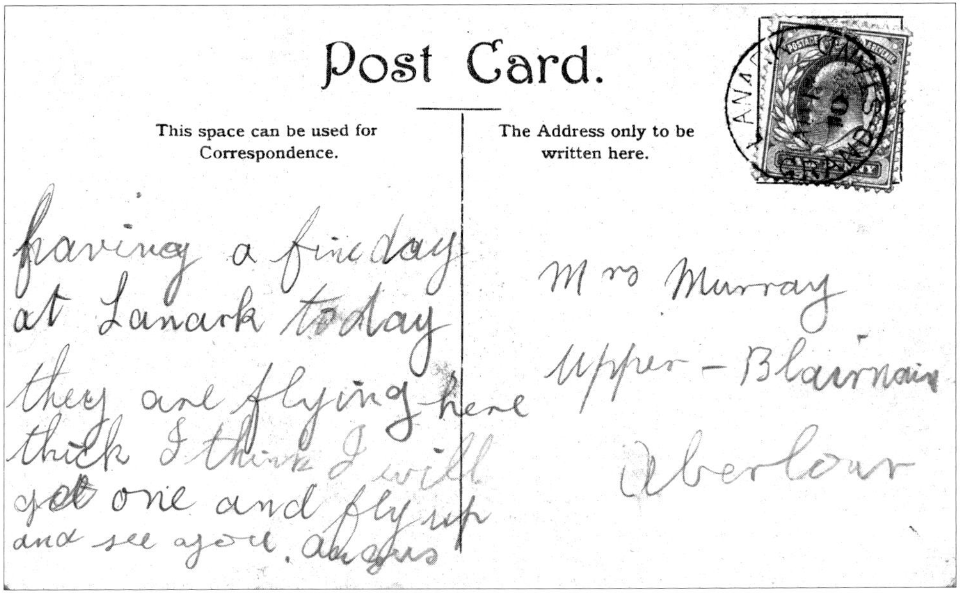
Post Card.

This space can be used for Correspondence.

The Address only to be written here.

having a fine day at Lanark today they are flying here thick I think I will get one and fly up and see you. Angus

Mrs Murray
Upper-Blairnain
Aberlour

This postcard was stamped on 10th August 1910 which was the day that over 50,000 people descended on Lanark. The postal facilities at the race course went through 25,000 halfpenny (the rate for sending a postcard inland) stamps during the course of that day and on the Wednesday they ran out of stamps. On this day a decision was taken to send 20,000 of the cards to Glasgow for cancelling. The Lanark Grandstand cancellation is much sought after. Even though thousands of cards were cancelled at the race course, few have survived the passage of time. What is also interesting about this card is the message about the impression that the aviators were making on the public and the fact that the card was of Delagrange who did not fly at Lanark. Cards such as these were probably unsold stock from the Hendon air show of 1909.

William McArdle (above) was the only Irish cometitor at Lanark. McArdle is shown left in a Bleriot giving the signal to the men holding the fuselage to let go, while they glance round to jump clear of the tail. The plane served him well throughout the competition for, despite a mishap on Friday 12th August, he managed to get his plane back into order and win the cross-country competition to Dunsyre the following day averaging 58.63 mph.

This card shows McArdle in Buchan's field, in Corstorphine Edinburgh, on Monday 8th August. By 12th August a card had been produced to record the event. McArdle had lost his way in a cross-country competition between Lanark and Dunsyre. The card also shows McArdle on top of his plane surrounded by a crowd of onlookers. The plane was undamaged and was taken back to Lanark by being towed behind a car.

Captain Bertram Dickson was a serving army officer at the time of the Lanark meeting. Cockburn and Colmore were serving officers in the Royal Navy. Captain Dickson was involved in assessing the military potential of various aircraft and at Lanark he was putting a modified Farman through its paces. One of the interesting feats was the transporting of a passenger weighing 14 stone. The weight of the passenger was not the problem but the lead ballast was too heavy and its ascent into the air was short-lived. The card shows Dickson's plane inserted onto a crowd scene photograph. Interesting features include the official photographer's booth and the adverts for the Caledonian Railway Company.

This photograph from the *Aero* shows Captain Dickson in his Farman. This plane was powered by a 50 horse power Gnome engine, placed behind the pilot. Planes with this arrangement were called 'pushers'. Later this aircraft had to be pulled back to the hangar using real horse power, by a Clydesdale horse after it crashed due to being poorly balanced. It was repaired but a new Farman modified by Wright with an ENV engine was used by Captain Dickson for the rest of the competition. The ENV engine gave more power than the Gnome engine.

Left: This postcard was one of the more credible scissors and paste jobs with an insets showing Captain Dickson's portrait and his plane. He was moderately successful at Lanark in that he won the *Glasgow Herald's* prize of £250 for the best British pilot. He also won several other prizes, including being the slowest around the circuit at the race course. He covered this at 21.29 mph. Surprisingly enough he stayed in the air.

FINEST FLYING GROUND IN THE COUNTRY

(3 MILES BY 2 MILES, FLAT.)

NEW FOREST AVIATION SCHOOL, BEAULIEU.

(Station—Brockenhurst, L.S.W.R.).

The School is now open and ready for Full Course of Tuition for either Monoplane or Biplane, £80. SCHOOL MACHINES.

PUPILS MAY BRING THEIR OWN MACHINES. Sheds will be provided for £1 per week. Ground FREE.

R.A.C. WILL GRANT CERTIFICATES TO PUPILS ON THIS GROUND WHEN PROFICIENT.

Principals - - - {W. E. McARDLE, ARMSTRONG DREXEL,} Certified Aviators British and French Aero Clubs.

Major Kennedy, and Mr Hogarth taking Drexel's altitude.

Armstrong Drexel, was one of the best aviators at Lanark. He was American by nationality, though in 1910 he was running an aviation school with William McArdle at East Boldre near Beaulieu, Hampshire. The school only lasted till 1911. Armstrong Drexel was the grandson of J.A Drexel, co-founder with J.P. Morgan of the world famous bank with the latter name. This world-wide bank is at the time of writing the most powerful bank in the world. Armstrong, however, had no interest in a career in banking, as aviation was his life. At Lanark he took the altitude record from Chavez by climbing up to 6,570 feet, at which height his engine was struggling. His record was checked by Captain Taylor. Drexel won a number of other prizes at Lanark including the *Scots Pictorial* Cup, the Lanark Cup and a cheque for £100 for a 67 mile flight. Of all the pilots who were at Lanark he was one of the most popular and successful.

This picture shows the impact Drexel's forced landing had on the people of Cobbinshaw to West Mosshat Farm to see Drexel's plane as he was making an attempt on the world altitude record on Thursday 11th August, but got lost, ran out of fuel and had to land. Drexel was very grateful to Mr. Wilson, the farmer, who lent him a bike to go to Cobbinshaw Station to telegraph Lanark Race Course for assistance. Help arrived and the plane was transported by Albion lorry to Lanark. As a thank you for the farmer's help, Drexel gave him his gold medal and his Goliath watch.

Marcel Hanriot was, at the age of sixteen, by far the youngest competitor and at that time was also the youngest pilot in the world. He flew his father's plane which Hanriot senior had designed and had tested earlier in the year at Rouen. The photograph shows the young Hanriot in his plane. Note the pilot is in the rear portion of the plane.On 10th August Marcel made a couple of rounds of the course then went up later to 1,300 feet, cut his engine and then glided. This was perhaps the nearest he came to winning a prize. He made another attempt to prove the worth of his father's plane on 13th August in windy conditions by taking up a passenger but could not stay up for long. *Lower left*: Tuning the plane. *Lower right*: Marcel with a passenger aboard.

Vidart never had his Deperdussin plane at Lanark, which unfortunately got lost between Boulogne and Blackpool, where Vidart was originally scheduled to make an appearance. Quite how a plane disappeared in transit seems difficult to comprehend. He borrowed Marcel Hanriot's machine and in it made a great impression on the crowds. The picture right shows Vidart at Lanark aboard the Hanriot. In the picture below Marcel watches from the ground as the plane is adjusted for Vidart.

Below: This illustration shows Marcel Hanriot, his youth quite apparent, standing behind the plane. The *Aero* described him as 'having the makings of a first class pilot'. Unfortunately Vidart was unlucky and did not win any prizes at Lanark.

Bartolmeo Cattaneo was one of the most popular aviators at Lanark. The picture left shows him flying in the direction of Tinto which was used as a landmark by the aviators. This photograph was possibly taken on Tuesday 9th August when Cattaneo was making an attempt on the altitude record. However, Drexel got up to 4,276 feet compared with Cattaneo's more modest 3,230 feet. Cattaneo put in several stunning performances. On Wednesday 11th August he flew 141 miles 188 yards without touching the ground and was up for 3 hours 11 minutes. This was to be the greatest distance flown in a single flight by anybody at Lanark. Indeed the flight was a world record. The same day in a different competition, he made a serious attempt on the speed record, achieving a speed of 56.46 mph.

On Friday 12th August Kuller's plane struggled around the course, the tail fell off and he landed in the fir plantation. Fortunately Kuller himself came out of the crash unscathed. Unlike Champel, Kuller did not land in the mature fir trees. Kuller again was uninjured, leading a somewhat charmed life. Kuller's lack of luck at Lanark contrasted with his success at Reims in 1909, where he had an incident-free show and won several prizes.

This scene shows a lull in proceedings with the members of the public not even looking at the sky. Often the crowds had to wait a long time for something to take place. Mindful of this problem the organisers provided a variety of entertainment including pipe bands and pierrot performers. Soft drinks were provided by Barrs and the sweet concessions were given to the Archibald's Battleaxe Confectionery Company. Barrs benefited a great deal from the Lanark International Aviation Meeting over 250,000 bottles of Barrs lemonade venue sold during the week.

Left: Wednesday 10th August was a red letter day for those attending the meeting. This card, which was not printed for the event, has been written on the front with the detail – Three up at 4.45 p.m. On the reverse of the card, the writer states that nobody has been injured. Given the unfortunate events at Bournemouth, where Charles Rolls had been killed, the public expected fatalities but this did not happen. The only person to fly a Wright Flyer was Ogilvie shown below.

Left: This is a fantasy card in that it does not show the crowds and it is quite obvious that it was produced to give people an idea of the types of plane that were to take part at Lanark. The most common aircraft flying were the Bleriot XI and the Farman. Other aircraft at the event included the Voisin, the Antoinette, the Tellier, the Wright and the Bristol Boxkite as well as individually produced aircraft like the Hanriot and Cody's Cathedral.

Audemars came from Switzerland and this card shows him in front his Demoiselle dressed very much as a gentleman aviator. To finance your flying either you had to have a private income or run a flying school. The plane shown in the photograph nearly did not make it into the air as while Audemars was testing the engine it caught fire. Cody rushed around from his hangar, extinguisher in hand, and put out the flames. The 'angry wasp ' or 'the infuriated grasshopper' survived to see another day.

Audemars tried to solve the problems of his aircraft by putting a larger engine in his Demoiselle. The confident manner of the gentleman aviator replaced by a clearly troubled man in overalls on the left of the photograph below. The experiment did not pay off and the Demoiselle did not take off so Audemars abandoned his first choice and went instead for the Tellier. He did not have any better luck in the Tellier as it landed heavily and broke its chassis (lower left).

The picture left gives a good view of the distinctive features of the racing Voisin including its front landing wheel. The Voisin company was to become one of the principal manufacturers of aircraft in France prior to the First World War.

Lower left: Champel's plane after it landed in a group of fir trees, referred to by commentators as roosting in the trees. He had started well in the competition with a good performance on the Monday, but despite getting his machine repaired, he never managed to make a comeback. This photograph shows *Lower right*: Florentin Champel by the tail of his aircraft prior to take-off on Wednesday 10th August.

Cecil Grace's start to the competition was not the best. On Monday 8th August the propeller of his drew up a mechanic's knife and took a slice out of his propeller, but fortunately the knife did not prove a lethal missile. On Tuesday 9th August he was involved in dropping dispatches – an orange on to a target. He missed the target by 23 feet. This exercise was devised by the military who were interested in how planes could be used to deliver both dispatches and bombs. Similar experiments were also being conducted that August in Blackpool.The photo montage lower right, was made showing Grace's Farman in profile with an admiring crowd below. It was Cecil Grace who was to walk away with the largest amount of prize money from Lanark. He won an amazing £1,950, almost a quarter of the total prize money. Amongst his successes were the *Glasgow Evening News* Prize provided for the race around Tinto. He was also involved in carrying a number of passengers on the last day of the competition including Major Lionel James, *The Times* war correspondent. He had to make a forced landing. Then he took up Professor Biles, but on landing with the professor, the propeller broke and the plane hurtled towards the enclosures. Fortunately the plane stopped in time.

Cecil Grace

Graham Gilmour was one of the British competitors who played a part in the Lanark meeting but did not achieve a great deal. Gilmour's finest moment came when he came third in a take-off competition. The aim of this competition was to prove how quickly a plane could get up into the air. For his efforts Gilmour was awarded £25. The other element that Gilmour seemed to excel in was flying around the race course area, much to the delight of the crowds, but he was not a serious contender in the main competitions. He delighted several people, including Mr. Moorhouse, pictured below climbing into the plane behind Gilmour, by taking them up as passengers but this would have stretched his machine to the limits as it was only powered by a 35 horse power Jap engine.

Here Edmond is shown sitting in his 'Bristol' biplane which was actually a modified Farman. Farmans were considered to be the most reliable biplanes and Sir George White decided to invest in this model after a failure with another French plane. Interestingly enough Edmond was a French aviator, but was chosen by Sir George White to fly the Bristol due to his knowledge of the Farman. However, the French mechanics were not familiar with the modifications that distinguished the Bristol from the Farman and so British mechanics had to be called in to assist with repairs.

The British and Colonial Aeroplane Co., Ltd.,

Builders of the

"BRISTOL" BIPLANES. MONOPLANES.

Aeroplanes built to Clients' own designs.

Propellers Specially Built for any type of Engine.

Rapid Delivery, Best Materials, Finest Workmanship.

Write for prices and earliest deliveries.

Offices and Works: BRISTOL.	Telegrams: "Aviation, Bristol." Codes: A1, A.B.C., and Moreing.	Flying Schools: SALISBURY PLAIN, and BROOKLANDS.

THE "BRISTOL"

is the BIPLANE which was specially chosen by

CAPTAIN DICKSON

for his successful demonstrations . . . . at the recent . . . .

ARMY MANOEUVRES at SALISBURY PLAIN.

This photograph shows Edmond posing on his Bristol biplane. The owner of the company making the Box Kites was Sir George White, grandfather of the present Sir George White of BAE Systems. He invested £100,000 in 1910 in setting up four different companies. The company behind Edmond was the British and Colonial Aeroplane Company. This company evolved into the Bristol Aircraft Company. This company was awarded the contract to build 61 planes for the military. These planes formed the nucleus of the Royal Flying Corps, later to become the Royal Air Force in 1918.

Left: The Bristol biplane and company vehicle at Lanark. The plane is being readied for one of Edmonds flights. *Below*: A Bristol plane belonging to the army on Salisbury Plain.

Kuller was the sole competitor from Holland and he had an unfortunate start to the meeting when his Antoinette caught fire on the train from Lancaster. He spent the early part of the week rebuilding his plane using spare bits and pieces.

From left to right, Audemar, Kuller and Cattaneo waiting for the wind to abate at Lanark.

On 11th August Kuller's machine tent pegged. His engine did not pull well, the wings caught the ground, the machine almost pulled up vertical and the propeller was damaged. However, Kuller was uninjured. He put his plane back together, broke another propeller then fitted a third. After that Kuller managed to do several laps at 45 mph. It was Kuller's lucky day as the previous night a plumber's lamp had ignited a petrol tank which his mechanic threw out of the hangar, thus saving the plane.

Lancelot Gibbs had two aircraft at Lanark, a Farman biplane with a seven cylinder 50 horse power Gnome engine and a Bleriot monoplane also with a 50 horse power Gnome engine in it. Relatively speaking the Gnome was more efficiently employed in the monoplane. This particular engine was a sound choice as it was technically the engine to win with at Lanark. In this photograph Gibbs is shown holding some papers in front of one of the planes, possibly his own although as far as can be gathered he never actually flew, Cecil Grace sits as piolot behind him. Gibbs who was involved in secret military activities with the Dunne 'swept wing ' aircraft at Blair Atholl in Perthshire, is credited as being one of the first aviators in Scotland. Although he did took part at Lanark but did not get any prize money. However, he played an important role in helping the other aviators such as Chavez by lending him his own Bleriot. He also lent Radley the Bleriot. Despite being unfamiliar with the machine, Radley managed to set a British record by flying at an average speed of 58.32 mph. Radley's success might have something to do with the state-of-the-art Gnome engine.

Cockburn was one of the first dozen fliers to join the prestigious Aero Club and showed himself very keen to promote flying. The photograph shows him flying in a Farman, though by 1911 he was flying a plane of his own design. Cockburn flew on Sunday 7th August at Lanark but little was mentioned about his performance. Subsequently he won the prize for the slowest flight on Thursday 11th August with a speed of 26.32 miles an hour. Later on in 1910 he was proposing a flying competition for the United Kingdom to match the proposed New York to Chicago competition. He like Colmore, was also involved in developing the Fleet Air Arm.

A fairly sparse crowd with Dickson's Farman used as an insert. The picture was probably taken fairly early on in the day before the large crowds had descended on the race course. Though the Farmans were made in France, it was an Englishman, Henry Farman, who built them for the French market.

This is a real photograph taken at the air show and shows the ladies staring intently in the direction of a Farman biplane. The camera has made a fine job of catching the fine Edwardian hats or should one say Georgian as George V had recently become king in January 1910 . However the photographer has had less success in catching the detail of the biplane. The photograph comes from a small album of photographs belonging to an Ayrshire family, identified by their Rolls Royce, which features in photographs in the album as coming from that area. The car was presumably parked in the large car park at the race course that contained over 1,100 cars, the largest gathering of cars that had taken place in Scotland by that date.

The photo booths attracted both old and young. This example shows a young mother and her daughters. The youngsters would be quite taken on with this type of souvenir.

This example shows an older gentleman and the number suggests some type of individual ownership of the photo that might have assisted with reordering from the company. On another example is a reference to the firm of Lees from Portobello near Edinburgh. However, Lees did not bother with a numbering system.

Top left: This card conveys in a comic way the effect that the Lanark meeting had on the members of the public. Crowded into a guest house and so tired with the excitement of the events, these gentlemen have gone to sleep where they have dropped. In the event the local guest houses did not benefit as much as they had hoped as many visitors came just for the day either by train or by car. Card courtesy Lanark Museum Collection.

Upper right: One of several romantic style cards produced for the mass market. Aviators were highly regarded and often mobbed, particularly by the fair sex. Cattaneo, the Italian aviator at Lanark was a favourite amongst the ladies of Lanark.

Lower right: Enjoyment was a factor that the organisers of air shows wished to promote as well as the venue itself. 'Having a high old time' as a theme for a postcard not only did this but promoted Lanark as the place to be in August 1910.

Tetard along with Barnes did not make it up to Lanark from Blackpool. The plane that is shown in the photograph is a Bristol Boxkite Tetard worked for the British and Colonial Aeroplane Company. In 1911 he was a test pilot for Sir George White and in February of that year was testing a couple of the Bristol Boxkites for the army at Salisbury Plain. This process was started by Captain Bertram Dickson shortly after Lanark in October 1910.

Below: The message on this is interesting in that it simply states that Hanriot, Cody and Grace were up together. Unfortunately the date is lost by somebody removing the stamp unsuccessfully. However, it is possible to work out that the event took place at 4.45 p.m. on the final day – 13th August, both Hanriot and Grace were taking passengers up at this time.

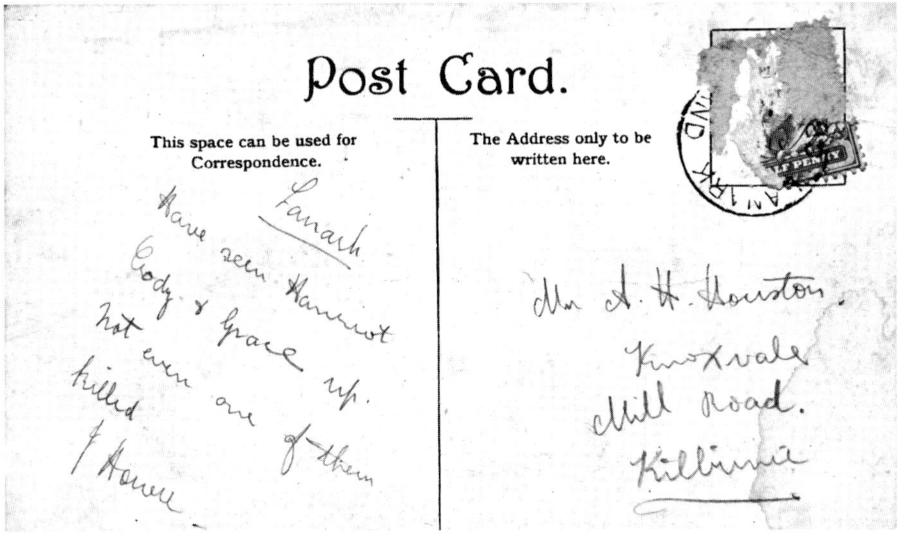

Post Card.

This space can be used for Correspondence.

Lanark
Have seen Hanriot
Cody & Grace up.
Not even one of them
killed
J Howell

The Address only to be written here.

Mr A. H. Houston.
Knoxvale
Mill Road.
Kilbirnie

Left: Colmore attended the aviation week at Lanark, but his Short did not perform well. It was originally lost in transit on the way to Lanark. In his frustration whilst he was waiting for its arrival, Colmore was reduced to watching wing warping in gnats! Though Lanark was not Colmore's finest hour, he was instrumental in founding the Fleet Air Arm down at Eastchurch. The navy was also not long in recognising the value of planes as is shown in this patriotic postcard showing a warship, Britannia and a plane flying up above. In 1909 the navy realised the benefits of aerial support and approached G.C. Colmore to get things set up. Before he made an appearance at Lanark G.C. Colmore had been involved in discussions as to the ranking of pilots as officers in the navy.

One of the awards that were presented to the participants was a gold medal showing Glasgow and a Bleriot flying over it. Ironically Glasgow was one of the places that the aviators never flew over. The Glasgow part of the tests for the aviators was abandoned due to inclement weather conditions. Photo courtesy Lanark Museum Collection.

The Clydesdale Hotel was used a the headquarters of the Lanark meeting for the whole week. The aviators met up here for a dinner after the last day of flying for a dinner with the main sponsors and officials. Cattaneo, the popular Italian aviator was carried shoulder high into the hotel. Other aviators were similarly greeted. Several aviators missed the dinner, in particular Chavez who had left earlier in the week for Paris. The dinner was hosted by Lord Provost McInnes Shaw, Professor Barr President of the Scottish Aeronautical Society presented the awards and prize money. Afterwards several of the aviators themselves spoke, (Cattaneo delivered his speech in French). Drexel was the star of the show and the centre of much attention

Captain Cody made a visit to Lanark in August 1911. He came to refuel on the northern leg of the Daily Mail Round Britain Competition. The French really dominated the race, but Samuel Cody was one of the best placed British planes. Instead of his flying cathedral Cody more realistically went for a biplane of his own design.Cody turned up to fly his plane in a suit and hat. During his trip around Britain, he stopped off to give lectures and was feted wherever he went. He was the only British entrant to finish and that was ten days after the French winner. Subsequently he set up a flying school at Hendon.

In September 1910 It was decided to sell the hangars at the race course, but the following month it was decided to make Lanark an aviation centre. Since the original hangars were not there or not suitable, Mr W.H Ewen , an organist from Glasgow opened an aviation school at Lanark on Saturday 6th May 1911. The flying school lasted just over two years until the council terminated Ewen's lease on 18th October 1913. Thereafter the site of the school was used by the military as a refuelling stop on the way up to Montrose.

Captain Barnard's Flying Circus made a one day visit to Lanark on Monday 14th September 1931. The picture above is of one of the planes from the event, possibly a three seater Spartan, that was the workhorse of Barnard's display. The full programme which the Spartan took part in covered about 2 hours. At the time the Spartan was one of the more popular planes used for acrobatics .

This plane was commonly used in the early 1930s for taking up passengers at air displays throughout the UK, but was particularly favoured in Scotland. It was designed by Sir Alan Cobham and was unusual in having a third engine mounted on top of the upper wing. The two Airspeed Ferry Liners used by Cobham were known as the Youth of Britain II and III.